SNAP SHOT™

Senior Editor Mary Ling
Designer Joanna Pocock
Editor Finbar Hawkins
Production Catherine Semark

A Dorling Kindersley Book
First published in Great Britain in 1994
by Snapshot™, an imprint of Covent Garden Books
9 Henrietta Street, London WC2E 8PS

Copyright © 1994 Covent Garden Books Limited, London

Picture credits: Gold Stag PR: 24tr
Photography by Jane Burton, Martin Cameron,
Mike Dunning, Neil Fletcher,
Frank Greenaway, Dave King, Richard Leeney,
Susanna Price, Kim Taylor, Matthew Ward.
Additional photography by Jerry Young © 6, 12, 13bl, 30b
All rights reserved.

A CIP catalogue record for this book is
available from the British Library
ISBN 1-85948-021-7

Colour reproduction by Colourscan
Printed in Belgium by Proost

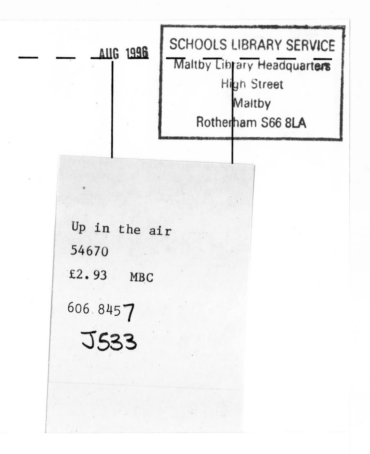
ROTHERHAM PUBLIC LIBRARIES

**This book must be returned by the date specified at the time of
issue as the Date Due for Return.**
**The loan may be extended (personally, by post or telephone) for
a further period, if the book is not required by another reader,
by quoting the above number**   LM1 (C)

Up in the Air

Contents

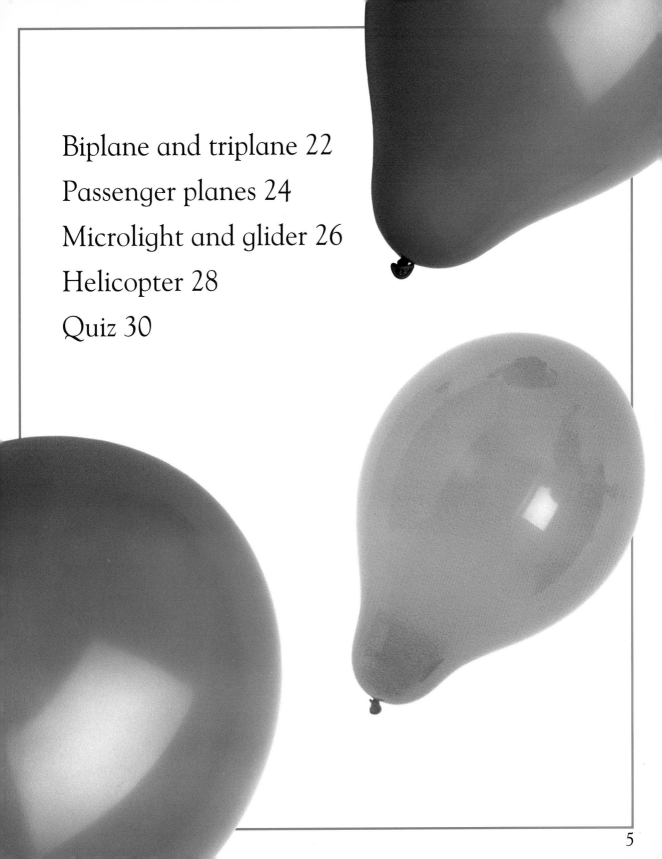

Would you

Do you
look into
the sky and
wish you could
fly like a kite or
float like a feather?

like to fly?

Flying creatures, such
as birds and insects,
have wings and bodies
that are specially made
for life in the air.

Why are your wings

These butterflies have brilliantly coloured wings that close up while they are resting.

so bright, butterfly?

Their wings help to hide them among flowers and are a colourful way of finding a mate.

What makes a

Insects do not dare take to the air if dragonflies are around.

dragonfly so scary?

These fierce hunters buzz past at terrific speeds, snatching bugs to gobble on the wing.

Where are this beetle's

wings?

The cardinal beetle has a secret. Under its hard shell, it hides a pair of foldaway wings. The beetle can flutter off to find food, or fly away from anyone who thinks it might be food!

How do hummingbirds hover?

Hummingbirds beat their wings so fast that they can hover like tiny helicopters. They hang in the air, feeding from flowers.

How does a bird

take to the air?

A bird flaps its wings to take flight. Air is forced under the bird as it flaps down, lifting its body upwards, high into the sky.

Wwhhooo hunts

Owls hunt
quietly and
swiftly in the
dead of night.

at night?

An owl's special
feathers muffle the sound
of its flapping wings, so it can
swoop down on prey in silence.

What whirls in the wind?

Some seeds
have little
wings that twirl
in the air, carrying
the seeds on the wind
to new ground.

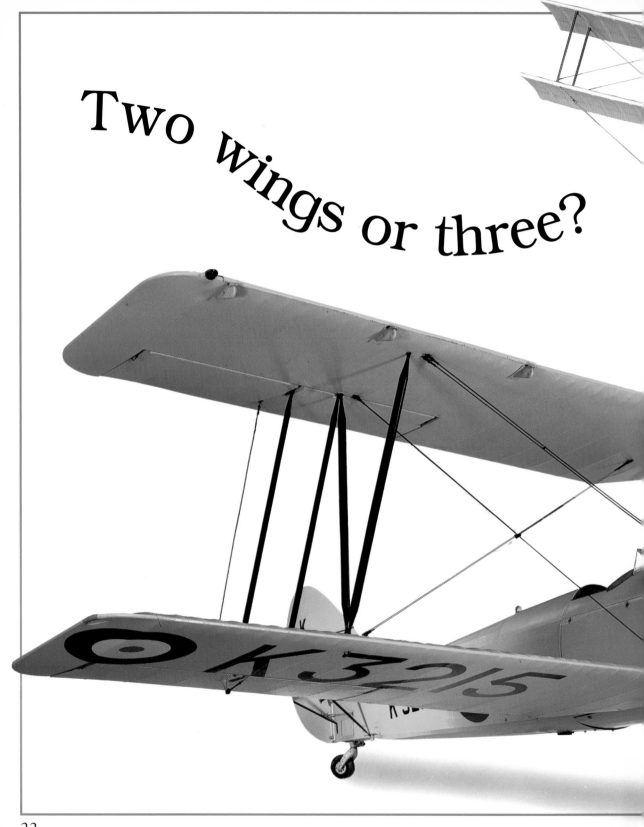

Two wings or three?

Many early planes had two or three sets of wings. They could zip across the sky, twisting and turning, or even looping the loop!

How many people fly in a plane?

Today's airliners hold hundreds of travellers and whoosh around the globe on jet engines. The first passenger planes used propeller power and only carried about ten people.

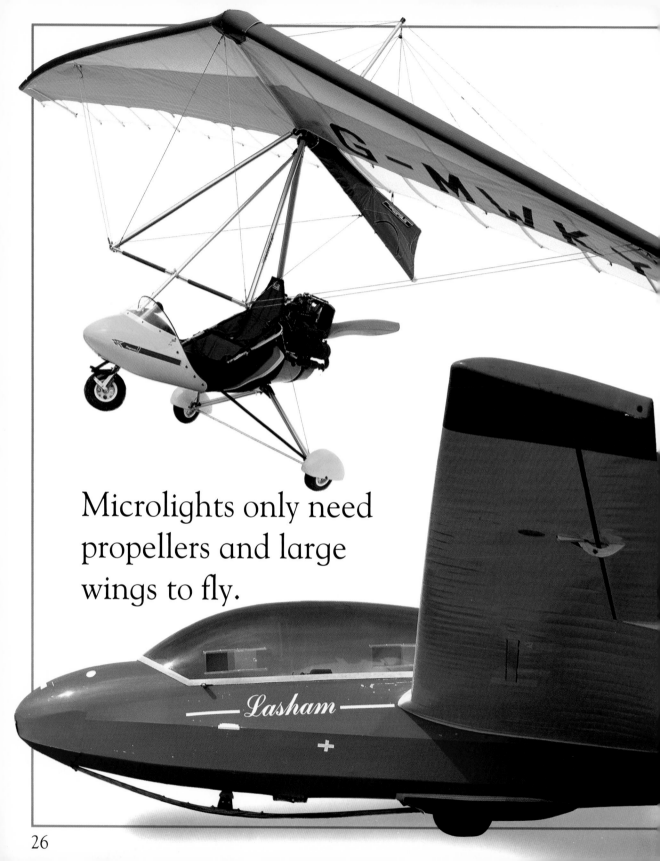

Microlights only need
propellers and large
wings to fly.

Do all planes need engines?

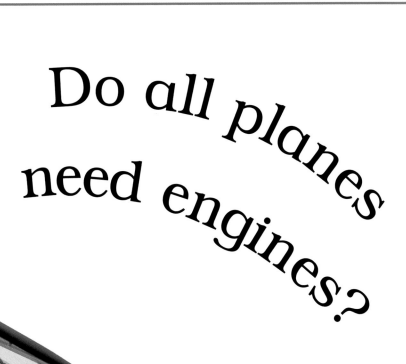

A glider has no engine, but very long wings can keep it swooping and diving in the air for hours.

How many ways

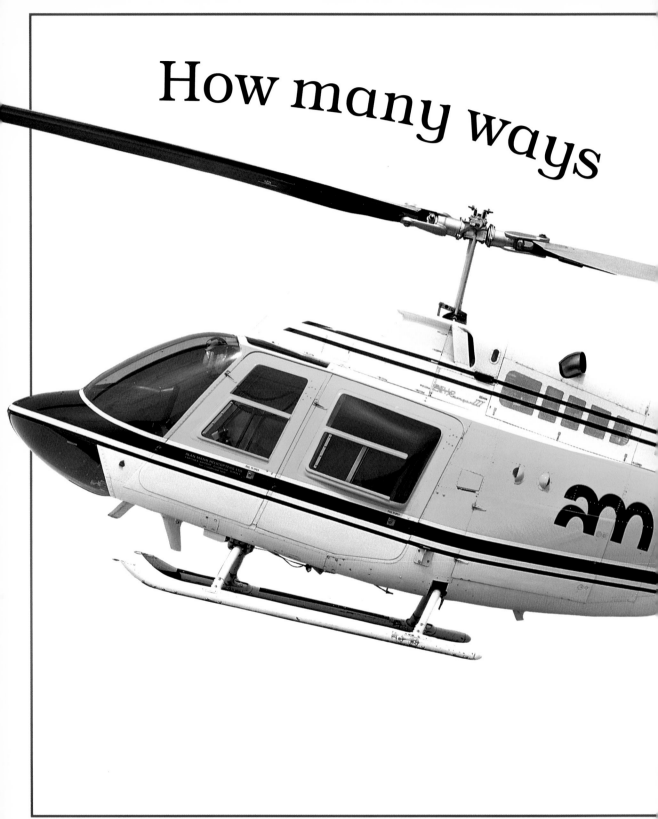

can a helicopter fly?

G-OAMG

A helicopter can fly
in any direction – even
backwards. It can also hover
in mid-air, staying perfectly still.

1

Whose wing

2

3

is whose?

4

5

6

Answers on page 32

Answers

1. Pigeon
2. Butterfly
3. Moth
4. Bat
5. Cricket
6. Owl